Inso Introverted and Ignorant

All poems are created by Joe Zux

Copyright © 2022 Joe Zux

All rights reserved.

Printed by Amazon Italia Logistica S.r.l.
Torrazza Piemonte (TO), Italy

41163930R00030

ABOUT THE AUTHOR

Grew up in the care system of the mid 70's to mid 80's, always told I'd never amount to much, labeled that bad kid, the one your family talks about in whispers. Thought I was just a bad kid, kicking off at school, not interested in having topics forced on me. Much more fun to learn what I wanted too. Eventually left care after countless beatings and lots of different schools, totally uneducated by society standards. Drifting from job to job, relationship to relationship with no real sense of who I really was. But I've always been a voracious reader and loved writing little ditty's and poems and poetry. Always kept it mainly to myself as it was my escape avenue. Anyway I'm now a lot older and wiser and realise the issues were down to un-diagnosed autism, not an excuse just a fact. So now I'm more sure of myself and just writing. I hope you liked what I put together in this book.

You pitiful excuse for a human being

Remember when I was sick in the morning
But better by lunch
Remember when you came on shift
Then sent me upstairs
So you could make me feel better with a punch

Remember your mantra
I'd better not tell
I hope your reward is waiting
I hope you burn in hell

A trouble maker
A bad egg
An uncontrollable child
A no hoper
A waste of time
All these badges I had to wear
With no one knowing me

So eventually it was off to Belper
To a home called Blackbrook House
Lovely Victorian building
Again Billy Bunterish
And told it was nice

You know what?
It was nice
A new family of Aunties and Uncles
Well that's what we had to call them
Trouble is I don't remember
I could have sworn there are no blood ties

We had the always happy Auntie
The laughable uncles
And the bastard one

Yes that's right Uncle Kevin
I'll name you Kevin Knowles
The uncle who batters kids

I remember you, you bastard
I remember each of your well placed punches
There to cause pain but not mark
The only lasting damage in my
And other countless kids head
Wow you really was something else

The lack of not adapting to my needs
Scarred me as good as any knife
What was the point
Why am I here
Being left to my own devices

Boredom

Always boredom the Bain of my life
Even when thing run smoothly
I reject the nice

So off we go to Stretton House
At first it was pleasant
Everything seemed nice

Had its own learning block
Felt it was feeding my needs
But apparently I was to intelligent
Back to mainstream schooling
Then inward creeping that boredom
Just like a disease

So then began the cycle
One school after another
Failing in every way
Learning nothing
Just acting up till I was expelled
I've lost count of how many

So there we have it
The label of a bad kid
Preceding me into every learning establishment

They'd already labeled me

Care(less)

Don't worry they said to my mum
It will just be like Mallory Towers
Just learning and fun

Here's a list of all the things he will need
Clothes, toothbrush those kind of things

All sold like a big adventure
Like a child's book
Boarding School dream

It was a dream alright
A fucking waking nightmare
Thrown into a world of social workers
Who didn't really care

It wasn't like that in the beginning
Stretton House, was ok to be fair

But that's not the start
That began at infant school
Me the uncontrollable child
Bucking at every rule

Fraught with boredom
Given the good old ladybird book
Went straight to hardest
Did I learn any new keywords
Did I fuck

Put into a regime
Where the first years are how to read and write
But I could already do that that

But there is hope one day
Like a mantra I carry with me
Don't hide away my younger self
There is still time for you and me

Where has that child gone

Where has that child gone
The one with the plastic guitar
And cap pistol gun

Riding his purple tomahawk
Not a care in the world
With brown hair
And a calf lick curl

Wearing a striped red blue jumper
Smiling on the school path
The one with the mischievous smile
The one ready to laugh

I sometimes still see him
Caught as a reflection in my eyes
On occasions I see him looking
It breaks my heart and makes me cry

A childhood that was taken
Thrown into a world of lies
Just for having autism
Sometimes this world I despise

But I know he's deep within me
Always watching as I take this path
Still inside laughing at nonsense
Still with me on this path

The world never bared down on him
He's safe with me inside
Oh how I miss his care free ways
In a world I sometimes despise

I wish you'd never had pain so you can make that final leap,

I wish I could lay with you, protect you while you sleep,

I wish the world were better and you was always treated right,

I wish I could guard you and keep you safe from demons in the night,

I wish you could understand me and know all I say is true,

I wish we were together as one but always me and you,

I wish you could understand I've fallen for you hard,

I wish you could understand I know my own heart,

I wish I could say the words to open up your heart,

I live here in hope and longing,
Knowing what I say and write is true.

I wish I wasn't crying but my soul screams out for you

I Wish

It's hard to explain how I'm feeling,
I'm scared this is all a dream and I will wake up and it's not
real.

I'm scared I've met the Ying to my Yang and it's not reality,
I've been searching for what seems eternity,
To match the music to my song.

I wish I could hold you and never let go,

I wish I could fall into your eyes,

I wish I could drown in your love,

I wish I could show you I'm here, you just have to take me,

I wish you could see how you make my insides churn with
my longing,

I wish you could see how your words have sent my heart
beating,

I wish the time we're together would last forever,

I wish I could just hold you and nurture you,

I wish that in your dark days I could forever be your light,

I wish I could show you how my words are true,

I wish I could make you understand I'd never hurt you,

I will wait for you

I will wait for you
Until the stars fall out of the sky
I will wait for you
Until the oceans bleed dry
I will wait for you
Until the sun stops to glisten
I will wait for you
Until the world has nothing left to listen
I will wait for you
Until the universe reaches its end
I will wait for you
Until time heals and starts to mend
I will wait for you
Because you are more than enough
I will wait for you
Till you knowingly return my love

Stop every now and again and look around you, take it all in.

Hold those you love and care for, because one one day you won't be able to.

Laugh, laugh loudly and don't worry who sees.

Listen to music you like and dance and don't worry who sees.

This isn't a test or a run through, life is a one go shot, so live it.

Try to make someone smile, it may be their only one all day.

Never be scared to ask for help, we all need a hand at times.

Don't follow to fashion, it's only there to make you spend and feel bad about yourself.

Look in the mirror, the reflection is you, and you are beautiful as you are unique.

Live for yourself as after all it is your life.

Always remember things can change in the blink of an eye.

Blink

Remember life can change in a blink of an eye.

What's planned for tomorrow, try to start today.

It may seem quite insignificant to others, but it's ok it matters to you.

Don't define yourself on expectations of others, be you for you alone.

What happened yesterday is in the past, try to move towards the future.

Not everyone is going to like you, that's ok, you're not going to like everyone.

Never allow anyone tell you not to change, that's how you stagnate.

People will either encourage you to grow and evolve with you or get left behind.

It's ok to be scared, don't be afraid to reach out.

I've learnt it's OK to not know what you want to do with life I've also learnt that doesn't mean you don't have plans.

It's ok to step away from toxicity regardless of who generates it.

Try not to judge others on first sight, you do not know their story.

Just the human race
Fooling with the last supper plate

So for me and you and others of our kind
Like the humans on the verge of extinction
We're losing the last grains of time

They cannot see
Anguish or pain
They cannot see
The innocence
Inside a kids brain

Said "you'd better believe it"
"A whole world's nuclear might"
But now it's too late
Your body turns to ash
No more feelings, thoughts or sight

The earth destroyed
Armageddon in a mushroom shroud
The darkest night skies
An everlasting radiation cloud

Cast your face high
Feel the burning wind
The cut as the scythe sweeps down
You have no body
You're not able to run

Slowly they descend
Freed at last
Riders of the apocalypse
Everywhere their shadow is cast
The horsemen return
From the pages of the past

It's just a shame
We tried to warn them
Now it's far to late

No Reprive

Fuck the world
Drop the bomb
Do you really care

Political imbeciles
Talking of trouble and strife
One false word
One press of the button
We all get the knife

Leaders and generals
All sat in bunkers on their asses
Banging away on computer keyboards
Planning the destruction of the masses

All just a political game
With people as chess pieces they play
Not realising each time it gets harder
With no option but to blow us away

They'll tell each other
When the time comes
"We're only defending what's right"
"We're only putting up a fight"
They're only deciding our plight

But.......

They're to blind to see
Children playing in a park
They cannot see
The fear in their eyes
As the world turns dark

Festie Time

Anticipation of the waiting
Is it too early to set off
Got my camping and care kit
Checked again and again

Time to hit the road
Arrived no hassle, tent set up
Wait for the gathering of friends
A festie clan combining for the weekend

Wristband on enter the show
Meeting everyone old and new
Watching the sound checks
Drinking a beer or few

Time for the bands to start
Dancing with abandon
Not a care in the world
Lost in the music and swirl

Singing along loudly
Its a massive combined chant
Old comrades, new friends
All lost to the sound of the dance

Sat round the campfire
Flames raging high
Laughing as a massive group
All enjoying the festival high

Free Streams

I feel like cancelling Netflix but I don't even pay for it
Apart from Strangers eating Squid I can't find much else
I wonder if they'll refund me, even though it's not my
account

I feel the same about Disney, It's just the Star Family Dad
But guess what, yep that's free too, see a theme here,
don't you

I want to cancel Brit Box, they're all eventually repeated on
ITBBCV, but I didn't start a subscription, even that ones
free

I want to cancel Amazon, it's totally past it's Prime
I'm glad I don't pay for that either so why do I sit here and
whine

Banish The Dog

Wanting to reach you when your doors are all closed.
When that dog day comes to visit and you've locked
yourself alone.
Doesn't matter how hard I pound on the door you won't let
me in.
I'm not going to give up I will keep on pounding until the
hinges give in.
Grab that dog and send it away, hold my arms round you
and keep it at bay.
Remind you with kisses, hugs and whispers that it's ok to
not be ok.
Grab all I posses like a banner shining bright, hoping to
warm you, you're not alone in this fight
Reach out I'll be waiting, all my love in my heart, banish
the dog days and make a new start.
When the dog comes sneaking back, let it know to slink
away, you've found a new pack.

No Crime

It's no crime to picket a line, it's what you forced me to do,
up until then I felt fine.
You can't tell me what I'm doing is wrong, it's my right to
protest with body, voice and song.
Had a chance to listen, to make it right, now we have no
choice but to fight
Using the MSM, what a cowardly move, we have other
outlets to voice the truth.
Shouldn't come to this in this day and age, it's like
reviewing a past history page.
The multitude classes, eventually we'll all wake and you'll
be out on your asses.
Your made up middle to keep you safe, you'll soon find that
is a waste.
You started it, class war, making sure you're richer by
fleecing the poor.
Your base is getting smaller with each passing year, you
even took over a working class party to ease your fear.
Fingers crossed it will soon be over, we can get back
control, you and your ilk consigned to a hole.

We need another path, one that's true
The time is here to stand together
We the masses must group and unite
It's time to end this bloody madness
It's time to gather, stand up and fight

Remember

Remember where you came from
The things you stood for
Wheels are turning full circle
We've all been here before

Thatcherism in a Truss
A mimic of the past
But still the same old values
Downtrodden working class

So time again to rise
We've beaten this before
But together we must unite
To fight of the Tory Whore

They will try to control the media
Brainwash us to turn against each other
But we must stand together stronger
As one, with our fellow sister and brother

We must not blame the striking workers
They who have no choice but to picket
Time has come to unite as one for society
As has gone before, we are all caught in it

Rising living costs to generate the profits
All for the top echelons wallets to thicken
Feed us on just enough scraps, lies and untruths
Hoping we swallow it, like a grateful chicken

The government only pretend to care for us
The colours Red, Green, Yellow and Blue
It's all just mingled messed up together now

Shhhh

You won't hear a sound
Not even a little peep
I'll be quieter than a mouse
Even a stunned startled sheep

Not one more utterance
No sound to make the needle tremble
Quieter than the bell of Old Tom
This quietness I am able

I will be even more invisible
Quieter than the silent of the night
Dedicated to the pursuit of nothingness
Like a shadow cast without any light

You'll no longer hear me coming
Not realise I've been and gone
Like a ninja in the darkness
But not hurting anyone

So finally I will have learned it
A lesson that will run so deep
As nighttime comes and passes
I'll shut up talking and let you sleep

Seeking refuge by the fire

Glimpses of the Gwragedd Annwn
Sprightly in the mountain lake
Taking tales to Annwn
To the king Gwyn ap Nudd

Enjoying my walking rambles
In the land of the red dragon
Feeling the wind whipping
The power, the beauty and peace

Mynydd

Meet at the cattle grid
We'll walk by the cobble wall
Follow the green lane down
Adjacent to the running brook

Follow round the bottom
Slightly up the rise
Footprint clear in the grass
St Michaels Chapel

Then wander towards the coast
See the crouching rock
Like a praying monk
Frozen forever in servitude

Waves smashing the cove
No smugglers rest today
No sign of the old jetty
The pilgrims path they made

Most western point available
Bardsey Island clear in view
Wishing I could inhabit it
Goleudy Ynys Enlli Lighthouse

To the top of Mynydd Mawr
The lookout still on top
Nothing to guard from
Just the passing gulls

Ignoring calls from the Gywllion
Trying to temp me from the path
Knocking on my door later

Knickers

Amazing to see our underwear, hanging together on the line

Blowing together and mingling, looking mighty fine
It's a bit like our relationship
Flowing along life's washing line
Pegged on it together
Hanging doing fine.

Ignorant, my greatest gift, my self protector.
Don't let anyone know you're aware.
So much easier to play at being an uneducated thicko.
People just have their guard down, unaware you
understand every word, action and motive.

Be careful when labels seem to fit, because it's not always
it.

So thank you for giving me Insolent, introverted and
ignorant, I shall carry them always as my weapons and
shields.

Insolent, Introverted and Ignorant

Still remember it well,
A badge that was given in spite,
Carry it proudly now I'm older,
Insolent, introverted and ignorant.

Love it, it was all about me, me, me,
Or should I say I, I, I.
Insolent, showing a rude and arrogant lack of respect.
Introverted, concerned only of my own affairs, inward-looking.
Ignorant, lacking knowledge or awareness, uneducated.

How foolish to believe this was me,
How stupid of you to see nothing of the real me.
Just a childlike mirror reflecting your own prejudices and beliefs back at you.
So self assured in your assessment of me that you wore the blinkers I made.
Wrapped up in your pseudo language trying to define me, without once actually knowing me.

Insolent, of course I was Insolent, shoved into a care system that didn't care.
Respect, of course you had no respect from me, as I was just returning what was delivered.

Introverted, well I had to be, didn't see anyone else looking out for me. Didn't see anyone else actually caring what happened to me.
Of course you asked me questions, but you'd already decided on the answers.
So yes introverted was the path for me.

Along The Highway

We all have a car to drive, a road to take to our destination, there may be many diversions along the way.

Sometimes you feel you've reached the end, only to find it's just a temporary stop.
So again you set off traveling forward, no map to guide the way.

At times you may find yourself at the same location.
This is OK as long as you're traveling forward.
Never travel backwards, the past journey can never be changed.

Sometimes you may find yourself on a roundabout not sure which is the right exit, don't worry they all lead somewhere.

Sometimes you stop at a red light and live in that moment.
Other times it's green and you travel straight through.

At times you will pick up passengers, some may remain with you throughout your journey, some will leave, some will be picked up dropped off and picked back up again. That's ok too, you will always have enough seats.

Screw Fucking You

You're gonna hear things

I'm not gonna lie
Don't judge until you hear it all
You don't know why
Think you know me
Wrong, think again
Think you got me covered
I'd like to know when
I'll keep quite for now
Really not worth the shit
If you action without knowing
Don't care, fuck it
After all you ain't me
You're not living my life
Anger, pain, frustration
Things cut deeper than knives
But I'll get past it
I always do
So next time I'm smiling
Screw fucking you

You have the problem, don't try to deflect your misunderstanding on me.

Why can't he just act normal, surely it's not that hard.

Bravo, now define my normal.
Is it the perfect family and 2.4 children?
Is it the going to the pub or club?
Is it the nice house with a garden and white picket fence?
Is it going to the cinema?
The beach?
On holiday?
Bustling markets?
Answering the door?
Ringing people?
You know social interaction?

But you know what? Fuck you, I'm me
You have the problem, don't try to deflect your misunderstanding on me.

I've got many different heads and coping skills that I let all you see.

But if you're quick to judge, you still don't get it? It's easy, fuck you, I'd rather be me.

Judged By Social Standards

It's not too much fun when no one gets you

Judged by social standards of norm
Fit into this box, act this way.
Do what society expects in the NORMAL way.

Well he can do a job, look he does it everyday.
Of course I do, you idiot. But you have no idea how hard it is to fight the urge not to do it.
You have no comprehension on the battle I face to answer a phone.
The fight to accept changes that were not defined in your original role. The things you take for granted are like a mountain to me.

But you know what? Fuck you, I'm me
You have the problem, don't try to deflect your misunderstanding on me.

Well he manages to go out.

Do I, are you sure about that. You have any idea on how hard it is to step over your own threshold and out of your space.

Look he went into the shops.

Yes I did, big brave me. You know why I managed that, well guess what I didn't manage it, internally I just wanted to get the hell out of there, and sometimes, I have no choice. I have too.

But you know what? Fuck you, I'm me

Daytime turns to darkness with only the glimpse of flashing lines and the occasional red rear eyes.

Some are tiring now, slumbering in their vibration, motion head.
Others are talking to loved ones, waiting for and hoping for, the journeys end.

I now have some one sat next to me, maybe we have stories to share, perhaps I won't say a word, just look out the window and see my reflected face just sit there and stare.

But eventually this journey will finish, every start must have an end.
Everyone finally meeting their lovers, their families or friend.

Blurred Trees

Blurred trees, green fields, pylons passing in the distance.
Blue signs, roundabouts, the route leading of into the
distance.

Bus noise, baby yawls, fractured conversation.
The symphony of the sounds,
All accompanied by tyre noise as the wheels go round and
round.

Overheard conversations, I'm not sure if Jeanette will ever
get that dress, or Jim will meet his onward connection.
Even if Steve will meet his friends and gets smashed.

Me, I'm just sat here wishing I did grab that drink to bring
with me.

Lamenting why the long distance coach has no USB. .
So that's it, WiFi off, Bluetooth off, screen dimmed low.
Disconnected from the world for a while, sitting in a
travelling bubble, it's own little reality show.

Here we are at another stop.
Few more people getting on.

Wonder where they are going,
Are they going home to meet loved ones, maybe they're
leaving loved ones behind.
Maybe their running to a new future, a new start, a new
time.

We all travel onward with each passing mile marker
flashing by.

Flickering Pictures

Flickering pictures blind our eyes,
Force fed controlled entertainment and media, unable to distinguish truth from lies.

Wireless popularity, this is now our price, our god, our goal.
Famous for unpacking boxes, unboxing our soul.

Staying in, no need to go out. All is good in the world, all provided by Bezos and his like.
Rivers of passing delivery vans, food arriving by bike.

Keeping up with Jones's is still here, don't be surprised or shocked.
But now it's judged on doorsteps, with a cardboard smiling box

Living with a government that only appreciates its own power.
Not bothered about the masses, we're just an unruly shower.

But still we vote and hope they're better,
Hoping red is no longer a shade of blue.
Still we keep on never learning from it, the fault is me and you.

Maybe one day we will awaken, put down our screens and avert our eyes.
No longer blinded by the flickering pictures, that control our thoughts, our life.

Now Jonny's rant is said, so goodnight

A Poem for Jonny

Murdoch and his masses
Beating down working class asses
Printed paper directing the classes
Jonny drinking beer and mulling what passes

Media monkeys making the news
Lies from a typewriter constantly spews
Directing the clueless and their views
Brainwashed until their thinking is askew

Now we have Truss totally brain dead
Spouting nonsense straight out of her head
Living a dream, leaving us in dread
Still people believe the bullshit they're fed

They should listen to Jonny more
He is not a darling to the media whore
He'll sing the truth of what's in store
Dissect their lies, leave them on the floor

Stop reading the press to see where you fit
Cast away the MSM Australian fed shit
Remove the blinkers, you can do it
See the reality, stop sucking Murdochs tit

Don't blame the workers who have to strike
Stop echoes of the 80's, get on your bike
Don't be stabbed by a new Thatchers pike
Ruled by a thinly veiled Tory 3rd reich

It's time to stand for what's right
Classes not split, but ready to fight
Work as one together with all our might

Sail the Carpet Sea

The bed is so big without you,
I can roll and roll for miles,
Climbing over pillow mountains,
Searching for your cuddles and smiles.

The sheet is like a sail,
Blowing the bed across carpet sea,
Charting a course to find you,
So again you can berth next to me.

I'm finding it hard to sleep,
No one there to watch over dream waves,
No reassurance fighting sleep demons,
No companion to be my brave.

Hiding under the duvet,
I know it's a safe place of port,
Monsters can't get through the fabric,
I know I cannot be caught.

Even though it's only one night,
Sailing across the bedroom sea,
The bed is too big to sail alone,
I need you here to navigate with me.

So until we sail together again,
I'm not venturing from the bed,
I've dropped the anchor bolster,
And will stay awake and read instead.

ACKNOWLEDGMENTS

To all those people who finally convinced me to start publishing and performing my poetry. Matt for getting me to actually go on stage. Derbyshire Social Services for giving me so much inspiration to draw from, would love to say it was all positive. To my son Cizz Real, should check out his stuff on Bandcamp. To my daughters, whom I love very much. To The Men They Couldn't Hang, the soundtrack to my life and also to The Newcranes who still keep me dancing. Lee Simpson for invaluable advice on the cover photo. John Latham for telling me to keep writing.

20 I Wish   Pg 38
21 Where has the child gone   Pg 40
22 Care(less)   Pg 42

CONTENTS

	Acknowledgments	i
1	Sail The Carpet Sea	Pg 10
2	A Poem for Jonny	Pg 11
3	Flickering Pictures	Pg 13
4	Blurred Trees	Pg 14
5	Judged By Social Standards	Pg 16
6	Screw Fucking You	Pg 18
7	Along The Highway	Pg 19
8	Insolent, Introverted and Ignorant	Pg 20
9	Knickers	Pg 22
10	Mynydd	Pg 23
11	Shhhh	Pg 25
12	Remember	Pg 26
13	No Crime	Pg 28
14	Banish The Dog	Pg 29
15	Free Streams	Pg 30
16	Festie Time	Pg 31
17	No Reprieve	Pg 32
18	Blink	Pg 35
19	I Will Wait	Pg 37

DEDICATION

To Aspen, Egg and Wren